The Fishing Lure

The Fishing Lure

BY

GREER ALEXIS BACON

Dedication

To My Grandfather

George E. Stokes

who served in World War 2

who was a part of second wave of Normandy

beach invasion in the 29th division. Years later

shared his loved of fishing with his grandchildren.

The Fishing Lure

The reflection of the warm summer sun was a promising sign of ideal fishing conditions. My grandfather, who spent twenty-eight months in Western Europe fighting Hitler's growing armies, left with a wound that caused him to limp and be fully dependent on a cane at the ripe old age of twenty-two. Now in his mid-seventies, Gramps, my nickname for him, often took me to a pond located near the Finger Lakes, hidden away from popular fishing spots. As a young boy, my gramps had spent many summer days fishing with his father. Fishing was dear to his heart, and it was important to instill that love for fishing in my heart as well.

My seventh birthday, which was full of tradition, fell on the 4th of July. My gramps – who truly loved our country – called me "stars and stripes." My mother was quite good about making sure the 4th of

July wasn't about BBQ'S; my birthday was celebrated as well and not forgotten.

As it grew closer to my birthday, Gramps took me to the pond to fish. We were fortunate enough that the weather held up and the rain in the forecast was nowhere to be found. The pond was full of ordinary fish. Turtles rested upon the pond's edge. And when we got to the pond, we could hear frogs leaping back to safety.

Gramps and I knew each other's routine. He would grasp the hook of the fishing pole as I bravely wove a worm on the hook. On occasion, we would get lucky and snatch a good sized sunny. But the truth was, we saw more tadpoles than fish. But Gramps enjoyed telling me of his childhood – fishing here with his own father, and how on the 4th of July as a child, his father and he took a row boat

and sat and watched the fireworks light up the summer sky.

My birthday finally arrived. I was excited to dive into my favorite cake that my mother had made for me – butter cream chocolate cake. Set up at Keuka State Park, our tables were covered in red and white plastic table cloths. As my family arrived, my pile of gifts grew. This was ideal conditions for a young boy who had made a wish list five months prior to Christmas morning.

When it was time to open my gifts, my family gathered around. Gramps was sitting across from me with a bottle of pop. Surely he didn't forget a gift for me… or did he? I couldn't remember if he had set his gift on the table. One by one, I started opening each gift. Many of them were new school clothes; others were action figures, and a brand new fishing

pole from my mom and dad. I was enamored by my new fishing pole.

In a loud, firm voice, Gramps got my attention. "Hey, stars and stripes, come and get your gift from your fishing buddy."

As I made my way over, Gramps reached for his left upper shirt pocket. With a big grin, he handed me a small wrapped gift box. I opened it and lifted the lid to find a hand-painted fishing lure. It wasn't just any old fishing lure. It was covered in thirteen horizontal stripes and fifty stars with the year of 1776 hand painted in the bottom corner. It was the American Flag. My gramps truly loved the idea that my birthday fell on such an important date, it meant so much to him. He was letting me know to instill the same values in myself, such as liberty, freedom and an appreciation of our service men and women.

It was a reminder of how America is the greatest nation on earth and how to not take that too lightly.

"Thanks, Gramps," I murmured but I didn't look up to see his reaction.

"You are very welcome." I could hear it in this voice that he was pleased with my reaction.

The next morning, while the sun was still a glowing shadow, I quickly finished up my oatmeal. I could hear my Gramps opening the front door and making his way to the kitchen. I didn't give him a chance to say one word.

"Ok, Gramps. Let's go!"

I was so excited to use my brand new fishing pole. But better yet, to use my favorite gift of all: my stars and stripes fishing lure. Gramps guided me step-by-step, preparing my new fishing pole for use. He carefully tied my new fishing lure to the line.

Gramps had enough faith to allow me to cast out myself.

As I slowly reeled in my line, I felt a nudge. It was like nothing I had ever felt before. It wasn't a fish. I could only see a trail of soft bubbles in the exact place where my line sat on the surface of the water. I continued to reel my line. To our surprise, the bubbles stopped following. A little narrow head rose up from the water. I stopped in my tracks. Without enough time to react, the snapping turtle bit down on my line. I could see the reflection of my new fishing lure fade away. My lure was gone as quickly as the turtle that disappeared under water.

It broke my heart; Gramps tried cheering me up by offering to purchase a new lure for me. I didn't want a new one. I wanted the one that was dear to my heart.

The future summers left me hopeful of one day finding my lure again. As the years passed, there was no such luck. Because of my deep passion for fishing, I became the proud owner of a fishing store, located in the deep valley of the Finger Lakes.

As for my Gramps, who passed his love of fishing onto me, he passed away suddenly when I was twenty-nine years old. Although it was a heavy loss, I knew he was in a better place.

Gramps had asked to have his ashes scattered at the pond. I took the urn and my youngest son with me to the pond. The day was a flashback to my childhood – warm summer air with complete peace. With both hands carrying Gramps' ashes, I was relieved when we reached the edge of the pond. Kneeling down, I dumped the ashes. The tears rolled down my cheeks.

"Daddy, it's going to be ok," my son whispered in my ear. Suddenly, he said, "Hey, what's that?"

Drying my tears, I tried to listen. "What's what?" I mumbled.

"There, Daddy. Over there," he pointed.

As the ashes washed away into the water, something shiny rested at the edge of the pond. I reached in carefully and picked up the object, and I couldn't believe my eyes. There, in the palm of my hands, was the fishing lure I had lost as a child. It still had thirteen stripes and fifty stars and the year 1776 painted on it. Gramps would have been pleased.

Many years have passed since that summer day. My son has grown up. He, too, has come to love fishing. As for the best gift I ever received, the lure sits behind a glass case at my fishing store where it won't ever be lost again but will stay forever in our hearts.

The End

The Artwork Process

T.D Smartgroupvn, the illustrator of The Fishing Lure, brings to life each illustration starting with a sketch drawing of each character with carefully adding the background. With great patience the artist adds water color paint to compete each illustration shown in pictures.

About the Author

"Stand up for what you believe in
even if it means standing alone..."
— C.M.

Greer with her three year
old Daughter Honor

GREER ALEXIS BACON, a
native of Westchester NY.
Today, Lives in the Finger
Lakes Region of Western NY.
Where she and her husband
raise their two children and
work full time. Greer has been
writing since 2001 where she

started with poetry. Then not until 2005, Greer started working on "Guardian, Where A Dream Is Challenged" her first published work. Today, she continues to write children's books. Stories that will touch children's heart as well adults alike. With help, to bring her books alive, T.D Smartgroupvn an artist from Vietnam. He illustrates each picture with the beauty of watercolor paints. Greer would love to hear from her fans like you! You can email her at: greerbacon@gmail.com

To many years of reading and writing,

Greer Alexis Bacon

Made in the USA
Lexington, KY
15 December 2018